First World War
and Army of Occupation
War Diary
France, Belgium and Germany

39 DIVISION
Divisional Troops
East Lancashire Regiment
1/4th Battalion
1 February 1917 - 7 June 1919

WO95/2577/2

The Naval & Military Press Ltd
www.nmarchive.com
Published in association with The National Archives

Published by

The Naval & Military Press Ltd

Unit 10 Ridgewood Industrial Park,

Uckfield, East Sussex,

TN22 5QE England

Tel: +44 (0) 1825 749494

www.naval-military-press.com

www.nmarchive.com

This diary has been reprinted in facsimile from the original. Any imperfections are inevitably reproduced and the quality may fall short of modern type and cartographic standards.

© **Crown Copyright**
Images reproduced by permission of The National Archives, London, England, 2015.

Contents

Document type	Place/Title	Date From	Date To
Heading	WO95/2577/2		
Heading	39th Division 4th Bn East Lancs Regt 1918 Aug 1919 Jun From 66 Div 198 Bde		
Miscellaneous	War Diary From August 1st 1918 To August 31st 1918		
War Diary	Abancourt	01/08/1918	15/08/1918
Miscellaneous	Battalion Orders By Lieut. Col. G.P. Norton D.S.O. Commdg 4th. Bn. East Lancs. Regt.	15/08/1918	15/08/1918
War Diary	Abancourt	15/08/1918	15/08/1918
War Diary	Calais	16/08/1918	31/08/1918
Miscellaneous	4th Battalion East Lancs. Regiment. War Diary From Sept 1st 1918 To Sept 30 1918 Volume		
War Diary	Beaumarais Calais	01/09/1918	30/09/1918
Miscellaneous	War Diary 4th Battalion East Lancashire Regiment From 1 Octr 18 To 31 Oct 18		
War Diary	Beau Marais Calais	01/08/1918	31/08/1918
Heading	4th Battn East Lancashire Regt. War Diary. From Nov. 1st 1918 To Nov 30th 1918		
War Diary	Beau Marais Calais	01/11/1918	30/11/1918
Heading	War Diary Of The 4th East Lancashire Regiment. For The Month Of December 1918		
War Diary	Calais	01/12/1918	12/12/1918
War Diary	Havre	13/12/1918	31/12/1918
Miscellaneous	A Cadre Group Calais	08/12/1918	08/12/1918
Miscellaneous	116th Infantry Brigade Order No 252	21/12/1918	21/12/1918
Heading	War Diary 4th. Battalion East Lancashire Regiment. From 1.1.19 to 31.1.19		
War Diary	Havre	01/01/1919	31/01/1919
Heading	4th. Battalion East Lancashire Regiment. War Diary. From February 1st 1919 To February 28th. 1919		
War Diary	Havre	01/02/1917	26/02/1917
Heading	War Diary 4th Bde E.L.R. March April 1919		
War Diary	Havre	01/03/1919	31/03/1919
War Diary	Blackburn	30/03/1919	30/03/1919
War Diary	Le Havre	02/04/1919	29/04/1919
Heading	War Diary Confidential 4th Battalion East Lancashire Regiment.		
War Diary	Le Havre	03/05/1919	31/05/1919
Heading	4th Battalion East Lancashire Regiment Month June 1919		
War Diary	Havre	06/06/1919	07/06/1919
Miscellaneous	39th Division	04/06/1919	04/06/1919

W0951/25772/2

39TH DIVISION

4TH BN EAST LANCS REGT

~~AUG - DEC 1918~~

1918 AUG - 1919 JUN

FROM 66 DIV
198 BDE

4th. BATTALION EAST LANCASHIRE REGIMENT.

CONFIDENTIAL

WAR DIARY

From August 1st. 1918. To August 31st. 1918.

VOLUME No..............

Army Form C. 2118.

WAR DIARY
or
INTELLIGENCE-SUMMARY.

4th Lan Lancashire Regt

(Erase heading not required.)

Summary of Events and Information
AUGUST 1916.

Place	Date	Hour	Summary of Events and Information	Remarks and references to Appendices
ABANCOURT	Aug 1st to 14th 1916	—	The usual training programme was carried out both the Brigade during this period. The future order was – Brigade to work with the 7th (Robin Hood) Battalion Sherwood Foresters and also the 1/98 Bn - 66 Division. Our H.Q. to Tothegill encampment from the 6th Lancs Fusiliers. Very sorry for Aug. very cold and through most, every evening to 6th. A.M. – The former leaving the Battalion to 6th. and others on leave. On the 14th the Bren alongwith the 7th (R.H.) Sherwoods and the 1/98 Division in view of the orders are attached to the 39th Division, to be called formation of an Officers' August as Staff — the 39th Division Officers' Training Dep.. The A.M. King Sanchez from the 9th Manchester Regt. and attached for duty. Bay spent in cleaning up the Camp ready for Inspection in the District. [signature]	[various]
	15th	—		

SECRET. COPY No.

BATTALION ORDERS.
By Lieut.Col.G.P.Norton,D.S.O.
Commdg.4t.Bn.East Lancs.Regt.

15/8/18.

1. The Cadre will move today to the new area,

   Entraining Station   BLARGIES.
   Detraining   :   CALAIS.

2. The Cadre will parade at 9pm. Dress;- Full marching order.

3. The Quartermaster will make the necessary arrahgements for Transport.

4. Capt. W.B.Topham, will hand over the Camp to the Camp Commandant and obtain a certificate that it was left in a clean condition.

5. The Quartermaster will arrange that each man carries Breakfast and Luncheon rations for the 16th.

(signed) F.R.Sewell,Capt.& Adjt.
4th.Bn.EastLancs.Regt.

Army Form C. 2118.

WAR DIARY
or
INTELLIGENCE SUMMARY.
(Erase heading not required.)

1/4th East Lancashire Regt.

Summary of Events and Information
AUG — 1918 — Cont'd

Place	Date	Hour	Summary of Events and Information	Remarks and references to Appendices
ABANCOURT	Aug 15th cont'd		Tents struck 5 p.m. — and camp finally cleared up — all camp stores being returned to Camp Commandant.	
		8 p.m.	Bn. paraded & marched to BLARGIES Station. Transport being sent to ROMESCAMPS Station during the afternoon with stores for Bn.	
		11 p.m.	Entrained for CALAIS, the train leaving at 2 a.m. on the 16th Aug 18. Whilst training in the Station hostile enemy aircraft were heard in the distance and our raid Alarm taken — bombs were heard but at a distance.	
CALAIS	16th	11-30 p.m.	After travelling all night arrived CALAIS — FONTINETTES Stn. The route being via ST. VALERY, ETAPLES and BOULOGNE. There was a halt of an hour at ETAPLES — from 8 a.m. — 9 a.m. After arrival in the Station at FONTINETTES the cadres marched through the town to the No.1 Overflow Camp, 4 Kilos from CALAIS on the DUNQUERQUE Road, nr BEAUMARAIS. Here the cadres were allotted tents. H.Q. of both cadres messing at the Princes Beatrice Camp and other officers at the 7th (Scottish) Divl. Officers' Mess.	
	19th		2nd Lt. J. R. Smith — double reported from leave, but as he is to transfer to the R.A.S.C. Mech. Transport, he was sent on to them on the following day.	

Army Form C. 2118.

4th East Lancashire R.A.

WAR DIARY
or
INTELLIGENCE SUMMARY.
(Erase heading not required.)

Summary of Events and Information
AUG 1918 - Cont.

Place	Date	Hour		Remarks and references to Appendices
CALAIS	Aug 17th to 19th 1918		Parades were held as usual, with route marches + bathing parades down to the shore. Good bathing when 40 min. march from the Overflow Camp – Physical training carried out on the sands. Work was commenced by the two Cadres – both under the command of Lt. Col. E.P. Norton D.S.O. – on the site of the new Officers' Training Depôt Camp. Work consisted of every kind of digging.	(3/1)
	20th	—	Staff of A.G generally getting the camp ready for occupation. Lt. F. Snowden reported for duty from leave, having been transferred from the 6th Hampshires. 30 G.s. + 3 marquees erected and camp is fitting out.	(4/2)
	21st	—	Nearer 3 clsp — Plenty of stragglers work in office. Lt. Col. Reade still spent in lasting stores. Ride to Ames from the Overflow Camp + fitting Camp in order, and stables traced out. Cadres occupied tents in this camp after tea. All the look now as the Sgt. Mess Officers Mess + cook houses.	(4/3)
	22nd	—	BEAUMARAIS. + to situated ½ mile south of it. 11.30 Overflow Camp was evacuated. O/C this Camp (Major Engineers to attack at along with an oth. Ceng. + R.A.)	(4/4)

signature

D. D. & L., London, E.C. (A10266) W.W 5300/P773 750,000 2/18 Sch. 52 Forms/C2118/16

Army Form C. 2118.

4th East Lancashire Regt.

WAR DIARY
or
INTELLIGENCE SUMMARY.
(Erase heading not required.)

Summary of Events and Information
AUG - 1918 - Cont.

Place	Date	Hour	Summary of Events and Information	Remarks and references to Appendices
CALAIS	Aug 1918 22nd		Work on Camp - After parade at 8am the C.O. invited working parties on shelter trench consts. Revolt a night out for splinters from bomb splinters - digging shelter of massive trenches for bomb splinters.	
	23rd/24th		Air-raid warning given. Enemy aircraft came over and air also bombs in the vicinity. Anti-aircraft barrage was put over CALAIS by the gunners for safety but no bombs were dropped on either district.	
	25th		All - Clear sounded. On the air-raid warning being given, all ranks occupy the specially dug shelter trench in the Camp Ground.	
	26th-31st		Work carried on daily by Cadres, engineers, and German prisoners - One Company of whom are sent down every day to Rouly-Dunes P.O.W. Camp, with escort, and work from 7-30am to 4pm (with 1 hour for lunch each day) - their work consisting of digging drains, camps, etc, in connection with the camp. Keen work in connection with the camp. The King's air project of Camouflage also manages the Camp to be temporary accommodation. Pending the construction of the permanent buildings - the times of the Sergeants' Mess, & Q.M. Stores complete Concrete Road to be laid at completion.	

M.M. [signature]

CONFIDENTIAL.

4th. BATTALION EAST LANCS. REGIMENT.

WAR DIARY. From Sept. 1st 1918. To Sept. 30. 1918.

VOLUME..........

Army Form C. 2118.

WAR DIARY
or
INTELLIGENCE SUMMARY.
(Erase heading not required.)

Instructions regarding War Diaries and Intelligence Summaries are contained in F. S. Regs., Part II. and the Staff Manual respectively. Title pages will be prepared in manuscript.

Place	Date	Hour	Summary of Events and Information	Remarks and references to Appendices
BERMUDA 1915 CAMPS	SEP			
	1		Church Parade. Instruction of Camp Captains - Officers under R.Q. Staff for having during morning. P.S.P.O. helped R.Q.	222
	2		Do.	222
	3		Do.	222
	4		Do.	222
	5		Do. Heat. Shaw and B. proceeded to BOPPES, and we a stand of having tent. Challegh from "Leicester Regt." taken on strength.	222
	6		Do. Lecture by Commander Kerr. Inspection last echelon Hooper.	222
	7		Do.	222
	8		Church Parade. Shoots keep. Started under Col. A. Blackburn	222
	9		Instruction of Camp Commanders - Officers under R.Q. Staff for training during morning. Brig. Seldon H.Q. Bom. of 4th Gen. also Regt. annex.	222
	10		Inspection of Camp etc.	
	11		Capt J.R. Sewell proceeded on leave to U.K.	222
	11?		Do.	222
	12		Do. Capt A.D. Prichard proceeded on leave to U.K.	222
	13		Do.	222

M. Morton

WAR DIARY
or
INTELLIGENCE SUMMARY.
(Erase heading not required.)

Army Form C. 2118.

Place	Date	Hour	Summary of Events and Information	Remarks and references to Appendices
BEAUMARAIS (Paris)	14		Underofficers moved from marques to huts.	1915
	15		Gymkhana	1915
	16		Institution of camp etc.	1915
	17		Do	1915
	18		Do	1915
	19		Do	1915
	20		Do	1915
	21		Do	1915
	22		Church parade	1915
	23		Instruction of hunt etc.	1915
	24		Do Capt. J.J. Sewell returned from leave.	1915
	25		Do Capt. Oates proceeded on leave to U.K.	1915
	26		32 Student Officers arrived from Rouen. Instruction of camp continued	1915
	27		Do Kilau Savage Bros? Martin made demonstration of Capt. R.J. C. Inkersgill. Capt. J.D. Richard returned from leave.	1915
	28		Instruction of Student Officers - Construction of camp. Grand Parade.	1915
	29			1915
	30		Instruction of Student Officers (Construction of camp) Mr Martin (Aim Sgt J. Stephens instructor (RE)	1915

Secret

C O N F I D E N T I A L.

W A R   D I A R Y.

4TH BATTALION EAST LANCASHIRE REGIMENT.

FROM ...1. Octr 18.. TO ...31. Octr 18

VOLUMN NO..........

++++++++++++++++++++++++++

Army Form C. 2118.

WAR DIARY
INTELLIGENCE SUMMARY.

(Erase heading not required.)

Place	Date	Hour	Summary of Events and Information	Remarks and references to Appendices
BEAUMARAIS (A+A15.	1918			
	1		Number of School Officers increased to 100 - instructors continue	AB
	2		Instruction of School Officers - construction of camp.	AB
	3		do	AB
	4		do	AB
	5		do	AB
	6		Church Parade	AB
	7		Lieut Rodleigh proceeded on Liason funderness (4N.2) held at Le TOUQUET.	AB
	8		Ordinary Routine	AB
	9		School Officers visited R.E. workshops at Les ATTAQUES	AB
	10		Ordinary Routine.	AB
	11		do	AB
	12		do	AB
			Capt J. Porter returned from leave. 2nd Lieut H.S.C. Goderych proceeded on leave to U.K.	AB
			Church Parade	AB

Army Form C. 2118.

WAR DIARY
INTELLIGENCE SUMMARY.
(Erase heading not required.)

Instructions regarding War Diaries and Intelligence Summaries are contained in F.S. Regs., Part II. and the Staff Manual respectively. Title pages will be prepared in manuscript.

Place	Date	Hour	Summary of Events and Information	Remarks and references to Appendices
BEAUMARAIS (ARDIS)	14		Ordinary Routine. Lecture on Trench Feet by Lieut. Wishart Reynolds	
	15		do. Lt Col A H King proceeded on leave to U.K.	
	16		do.	
	17		do. Lieut. Knatleigh admitted to Hospital	
	18		do.	
	19		do.	
	20		do. Parade.	
	21		Church Parade. Lieut Col. J.F. Horton D.S.O. relinquished command of the Battalion and proceeded to 15th (S.) Bn. East Yorks Regt.	
	22		Ordinary Routine. Capt. J. Penner M.C proceeded on leave to U.K. Lecture on Gas N.C.O by R.E.	
	23		do. Visit of Brig. Gen. Duffus CMG.	
	24		do.	
	25		do. Capt J.B.C. Oates returned from leave	
	26		do. Capt A.S.C. Fothergill returned from leave	
	27		Church Parade. Capt. R.H. King returned from leave	
	28		Ordinary Routine. Lt. Cholleigh returned from Hospital	

Army Form C. 2118.

WAR DIARY
or
INTELLIGENCE SUMMARY.
(Erase heading not required.)

Instructions regarding War Diaries and Intelligence Summaries are contained in F. S. Regs., Part II. and the Staff Manual respectively. Title pages will be prepared in manuscript.

Place	Date	Hour	Summary of Events and Information	Remarks and references to Appendices
Beauchamps Calais	Oct. 29.		Ordinary Routine. Lecture by Major Pickie.	A.P.P.C.
	30.		Ordinary Routine. 2nd Lt. A.K.M.C.W. Savory D.S.O. 2.Yorks. Rgt. took over a joined Unit and assumed command of the Battalion.	A.P.P.C.
	31.		Ordinary Routine.	A.P.P.C.

CONFIDENTIAL.

4TH BATTN. EAST LANCASHIRE REGT.

WAR DIARY.

FROM NOV. 1ST 1918. TO Nov. 30TH 1918.

VOLUME

Army Form C. 2118.

WAR DIARY
INTELLIGENCE SUMMARY.
(Erase heading not required.)

Instructions regarding War Diaries and Intelligence Summaries are contained in F.S. Regs., Part II. and the Staff Manual respectively. Title pages will be prepared in manuscript.

Place	Date	Hour	Summary of Events and Information	Remarks and references to Appendices
Beau Marais Calais	1/9/18		Ordinary Routine	A.Q.1.C.
	2/9/18		Ordinary Routine	A.Q.1.C.
	3/9/18		Church Parade. — Capt. Brown M.C. reported from Lewis Gun Course at G.H.Q. L.G. School le Torquet	A.Q.1.C.
	4/9/18		Ordinary Routine.	A.Q.1.C.
	5/9/18		Ordinary Routine	A.Q.1.C.
	6/9/18		Ordinary Routine. — Lectures by Capt. FitzGerald (Intelligence) and Lt. Chudleigh. (F.A.A.S.Capt)	A.Q.1.C.
	7/9/18		Ordinary Routine.	A.Q.1.C.
	8/9/18		Ordinary Routine. — Lecture by Capt. Page (Monday).	A.Q.1.C.
	9/9/18		Ordinary Routine	A.Q.1.C.
	10/9/18		Church Parade	A.Q.1.C.
	11/9/18		Ordinary Routine	A.Q.1.C.
	12/9/18		Ordinary Routine. — Capt. Brown M.C. left 15th for leave in France.	A.Q.1.C.
	13/9/18		Ordinary Routine.	A.Q.1.C.
	14/9/18		Ordinary Routine.	A.Q.1.C.
	15/9/18		Ordinary Routine.	A.Q.1.C.
	16/9/18		Ordinary Routine. — Capt. Brown M.C. returned from leave.	A.Q.1.C.
	17/9/18		Church Parade.	A.Q.1.C.
	18/9/18		Ordinary Routine	A.Q.1.C.
	19/9/18		Ordinary Routine	A.Q.1.C.
	20/9/18		Ordinary Routine	A.Q.1.C.
	21/9/18		Ordinary Routine	A.Q.1.C.
	22/9/18		Ordinary Routine	A.Q.1.C.
	23/9/18		Ordinary Routine	A.Q.1.C.
	24/9/18		Church Parade	A.Q.1.C.
	25/9/18		Ordinary Routine	A.Q.1.C.

Wednesday 4/9/18

Army Form C. 2118.

WAR DIARY
INTELLIGENCE SUMMARY.
(Erase heading not required.)

Instructions regarding War Diaries and Intelligence Summaries are contained in F. S. Regs., Part II. and the Staff Manual respectively. Title pages will be prepared in manuscript.

Place	Date	Hour	Summary of Events and Information	Remarks and references to Appendices
Beaumarais Calais	November			
	25th		Orderly Routine.	A.C.I.R.
	26th		Orderly Routine.	A.C.I.R.
	27th		Orderly Routine.	A.C.I.R.
	28th		Orderly Routine.	A.C.I.R.
	29th		Orderly Routine.	A.C.I.R.
	30th		Orderly Routine. — Capt. A.S.C. F. Stagall 6th S.C. Lanc. For: attd 4/7/5 "E Lanc. Rgt. proceeded to H.Q. 5th Army on appointment as education officer.	A.C.I.R

Majourity H/L1

C O N F I D E N T I A L.

WAR DIARY.

OF THE

4Th. EAST LANCASHIRE REGIMENT.

FOR THE

MONTH OF.

D E C E M B E R, 1918.

Army Form C. 2118.

4th East Lanc Regt

WAR DIARY
or
INTELLIGENCE SUMMARY.
(Erase heading not required.)

Instructions regarding War Diaries and Intelligence Summaries are contained in F.S. Regs., Part II and the Staff Manual respectively. Title pages will be prepared in manuscript.

Place	Date	Hour	Summary of Events and Information	Remarks and references to Appendices
Cairo	Dec 1		Usual Routine	
"	2		" "	
"	3		" "	
"	4		" "	
"	5		" "	
"	6		" "	
"	7		" "	
"	8		" "	
"	9		Entrained for Havre at 3-0 p.m. In train en route for Havre	
"	10		" "	
"	11		Detrained at 7-0 p.m. at Havre. Marched to No 2 Rest Camp	
"	12		Movement of stores to Camp. Usual Routine	
Havre	13		Church Parade voluntary. Usual Routine	
"	14		Lt Col Lugsden took command Brigade	
"	15		Cadre took up Draft-conducting duties from Stephen to No 7 Rest-Camp Section A. Lt Col Kenny relinquished command of Brigade and returned to unit	

DECEMBER 1918   4¹. Bn. East Lanc Regt.

Army Form C. 2118.

WAR DIARY
INTELLIGENCE SUMMARY.
(Erase heading not required.)

Place	Date	Hour	Summary of Events and Information	Remarks and references to Appendices
Havre	Dec 18	—	Draft conducting from Station to No 1 Rest Camp - Section A.	
—	19	—	2/Lt Topham Rejoined Unit.	
—	20	—	Ditto – Capt Brown MC, H. OR reported to No 1 Rest Camp for duty	
—	21	—	Ditto	
—	22	—	Ditto	
—	23	—	Ditto. Capt Bennett G. MC. reported to No 1 Rest Camp for duty	
—	24	—	Ditto Cadre moved to No 1 Rest Camp. Leave transport.	
—	25	—	Capt Brown MC. and 2/Lt Topham proceeded to UK on leave	
—	26	—	Cadre took over duties of demobilization at No 1 Rest Camp X Section	
—	27	—	usual duties. Camp routine.	
—	28	—	ditto	
—	29	—	ditto	
—	30	—	Capt + J/Colwell returned unit. Capt Prichard proceeded to UK on leave	
—	31	—	ditto from agriculture course Cambridge.	
—		—	ditto	

To:-
" A " Cadre Group Calais.

A.21.

8-12-18.

Communications wire W.11411. dated to-day begins. Move the following Cadre Battalions to Havre for duty in Demobilization Embarkation Camp. They are required at once. 18th. 23rd. and 25th. Northd. Fus. 13th. Gloucesters. 14th. H.L.I. 7th. Sherwood Foresters. 4th. East Lancs. An Officer will be put to Command the Embarkation Camp as soonas possible. Ends. For Action. Addressed 197 Infe Bde. and "A" Cadre Group. Repeated 116 Infy Bde.and G.S. Reference 39/472/A. dated 1-12-18.

From 39th.Division. " A "

COPY.

116TH. INFANTRY BRIGADE ORDER NO. 252.

21-12-1918.

1. (a) The undermentioned Battalions less Transport, will move on Monday
      the 23rd. inst. to No.1 Rest Camp, Section " A "
      Move to be completed by 12. noon.
            4th. Battn East Lancs.
            7th. Battn. Sherwood Foresters.
            14th. Battn. H.L. Infantry.

   (b) The 18th. Battn. Northd. Fus. less Transport will move on the same
      date to No. 1. Rest Camp Section. " B "
      Move to be completed by 12. noon.

2. Each Battn. will send forward their Q.M. or a senior N.C.O. on the 22nd
   to take over accomodation.

3. Transport and Officers charges will be left in their present location,
   there being no accomodation for them at NO.1. Rest Camp.

4. Arrangements for moving of kit and baggage will be notified to Officers
   Commanding by the Brigade Transport Officer.

5. A certain number of Officers, N.C.Os. and men will be left behind by
   each Battn. in No.2. Rest Camp to provide permanent guides and escorts
   for duty at the GARE MARITIME.

                                    Signed C.O. Bolton.

                                            Captain
                                         A/Brigade Major.

Copy No.1 TO 4th. E.Lancs.   116 Infantry Brigade.

CONFIDENTIAL.

WAR DIARY.

4th. BATTALION EAST LANCASHIRE REGIMENT.

From.. 1.1.19. —————————— To... 31.1.19. ——————————

117th Inf. Bde.

Army Form C. 2118.

WAR DIARY
INTELLIGENCE SUMMARY.
(Erase heading not required.)

Place	Date	Hour	Summary of Events and Information	Remarks and references to Appendices
HAVRE	JAN.1919 1-28	—	No. 1 Reception Camp — receiving troops for demobilisation	
"	29-31		No. 1 Despatching Camp — despatching troops for demobilisation	

Bolton? Major

CONFIDENTIAL.

4th. BATTALION EAST LANCASHIRE REGIMENT.

WAR DIARY.

FROM February 1st. 1919. TO February 28th. 1919.

Army Form C. 2118.

WAR DIARY
—or—
INTELLIGENCE-SUMMARY.
(Erase heading not required.)

Instructions regarding War Diaries and Intelligence Summaries are contained in F. S. Regs., Part II. and the Staff Manual respectively. Title pages will be prepared in manuscript.

Place	Date	Hour	Summary of Events and Information	Remarks and references to Appendices
HAVRE	FEB 1-7	-	Work continued at No 1 Despatching Camp Commanding Officer returned from leave to U.K. 15/2/1917	
	18		Moved from No 1 Despatching Camp to Cinder City Camp for duty at SOQUENCE STATION this convoy of ratings into from Italy. They and some few stragglers were sending them to be section camps.	
	21		Capt L Rose sent home to hospital suffering from Myocarditis Rheumatism. 2/Lieut Stanley R.E. attached for duty with 9th Pioneers Yorkshire Regiment. Commanding Officer took over command of H.Q. & Nos. Commanding Officer down by reason Brigade Commander being involved in engines to a fire.	
	25		Stephens dangerously who had escaped from No 1 Personnel Camp, arrested by the Pioneer Sergt Major who was concerned by the a/c M.P. Beautifully shot by four Mails Confusion on consequence which Capt H.E. Stansbury being attacked to P.P.7 Personnel Camp 2nd class taking the place	

War Diary
4th Bn E.L.R.
March & April
1914

WAR DIARY

INTELLIGENCE SUMMARY.

(Erase heading not required.)

Place	Date	Hour	Summary of Events and Information	Remarks and references to Appendices
HAVRE	1/5		Cams employed at SOQUENCE PLATEAU STATION for duty in meeting troops hospital ships and trains from Italy for demobilisation.	
	23			
	12		203489 Sgt E Been Commended for promptness in helping to	
			arrest a deserter thereafter at Soquence on 26/2/19.	
			(Brigade Routine Order p 55 - 15/2/19)	
	13		Capt R.W. Railton proceeded on leave to UK	
	15		Capts & Lors J Beard NC proceeded on leave to UK	
	24		Capt H.D. Packham transferred to base establishment for demobilisation. Capt R.W. Hay returned from leave to UK	
	28		Capt H.J. Brown NC had completed his moving to a few ...	
	29		Officers inventories	
	31		Capts & Lors J Beard NC returned from leave to UK.	

April 1919

WAR DIARY
or
INTELLIGENCE SUMMARY.

(Erase heading not required.)

Army Form C. 2118.

4 E Lanc Rgt

46 T.
1 vol

Place	Date	Hour	Summary of Events and Information	Remarks and references to Appendices
BLACKBURN	3rd		The colours of the Bn. were received from the Parish Church at Blackburn and taken to our unknown destination to the order of Lt. Col. F.D. Robinson V.D. Late O.C. 1/4 East Lancashire Regt.	No.
LE HAVRE	12th		Capt F.R. Sewell proceeded to U.K. on leave	No.
LE HAVRE	14th		Capt H.I. Brown. M.C. 4th East Lancs and Lt A.A. Walmesley 11th London Regt. proceeded for demobilisation.	Yes
LE HAVRE	19th		Capt & Adjt F.R. Sewell returned for duty	No
LE HAVRE	22nd		2/Lt R.L. Starkey 18th London Regt proceeded for duty to H.Q. 98th Brigade	No
LE HAVRE			4 E. Lanc Regt passed to 117th Inf Bde.	No

W Sharples Lt Col
Cmdg 4 E Lanc

WAR DIARY

CONFIDENTIAL

4th. BATTALION

EAST LANCASHIRE REGIMENT

Month   MAY   1919.

Army Form C. 2118.

WAR DIARY
or
INTELLIGENCE SUMMARY.
(Erase heading not required.)

4TH BATT
EAST LANCASHIRE
REGIMENT

No. ....
Date ....

Instructions regarding War Diaries and Intelligence Summaries are contained in F.S. Regs., Part II. and the Staff Manual respectively. Title pages will be prepared in manuscript.

Place	Date	Hour	Summary of Events and Information	Remarks and references to Appendices
Le Havre	3.5.19		Lt Col. R W Savory DSO proceeded on leave to U.K.	Appx
			2/Lt R Evans proceeded on leave to U.K.	Appx
Le Havre	5.5.19		Capt & Adjt F R Sewell proceeded to U.K. for demobilisation	Appx
			Capt R H King assumed duties of A/Adjt	Appx
Le Havre	10.5.19		2/Lt R Evans returned from leave	Appx
Le Havre	19.5.19		Advance party from 39th Division that the Cadre is to be demobilised in France.	Appx
Le Havre	23.5.19		2/Lt G H Soper rejoined the Cadre from hospital showing water in U.K.	Appx
Le Havre	31.5.19		Lt Col. R W Savory DSO returned from leave in U.K.	Appx

W W Savory

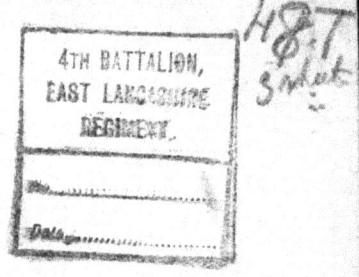

WAR   DIARY

CONFIDENTIAL

4th. BATTALION

EAST LANCASHIRE REGIMENT

MONTH   JUNE   1919

Army Form C. 2118.

4TH BATTALION,
EAST LANCASHIRE
REGIMENT.

No.............
Date:............

WAR DIARY
or
INTELLIGENCE SUMMARY.
(Erase heading not required.)

Instructions regarding War Diaries and Intelligence
Summaries are contained in F. S. Regs., Part II.
and the Staff Manual respectively. Title pages
will be prepared in manuscript.

Place	Date	Hour	Summary of Events and Information	Remarks and references to Appendices
Havre	6.6.19		Farewell letter from Brig. Genl. J. Hasselton Hall for distribution to troops received.	Appx
Havre	7.6.19		The Cadre moved to Concentration Camp for demobilising.	Appx

Havre Whitworth RMcN
7/6/19 Cmdg 4 E. Lanc Rgt.

39TH DIVISION.

Farewell and   Good Luck.

"Auld Lang Syne".

Officer Commanding

4th, EAST LANCASHIRE REGIMENT
....

1.   On the disbandment of the Division and demobilisation of the last of its 100 N.C.Os and men, I wish to thank you personally for the great loyalty you have displayed by remaining to the last, and sticking to your work in assisting demobilisation work through some very trying times.

2.   Though you have seen hundreds and thousands being demobilised and passing through your hands on their way to get started ahead of you in Civil Employment, yet you, who have been especially selected as one of our best and least able to be spared, and whose chances of the best appointments in Civil Life seemed to be slipping by, worked hard, uncomplainingly, and in the most exemplary spirit, knowing that your services were still essential to us in France.

3.   You now have the great moral satisfaction of knowing that you are one of those who have played the game to the bitter end.   I trust that you personally will meet with some material reward in Civil Life as a compensation for this final act of devotion to duty and display of utmost loyalty.

4.   I am proud to have had you, and such men as you, under my Command.   The best of luck and may you in your future career be prosperous and happy.

ROUEN.
4th June 1919.

J. Hamilton Hall

Brigadier-General,
Commanding 39th Division.

www.ingramcontent.com/pod-product-compliance
Lightning Source LLC
Chambersburg PA
CBHW081248170426

43191CB00037B/2085